REAL-LIFE MONSTERS

CREEPY, CRAWLY CREATURES

THE WORLD'S WEIRDEST SPIDERS AND BUGS

Thanks to the creative team:

Senior Editor: Alice Peebles

Designer: Lauren Woods and
collaborate agency

First published in Great Britain in 2015

by Hungry Tomato Ltd

PO Box 181

Edenbridge

Kent, TN8 9DP

A CIP catalogue record for this book is available
from the British Library.

ISBN 978-1-910684-19-1

Printed and bound in China

Discover more at
www.hungrytomato.com

REAL-LIFE MONSTERS
CREEPY, CRAWLY CREATURES

By Matthew Rake

Illustrated by Simon Mendez

HUNGRY TOMATO™

CONTENTS

Small is beautiful, they say. But that's not necessarily so in the animal kingdom.

Welcome to the world of tiny terrors and mini-monsters. Don't let their size fool you – these are some of the most fearsome, poisonous and downright revolting creatures on Earth.

Take the green-banded broodsac – it's a flatworm and it's quite obnoxious. It spends its entire life crawling around the insides of snails or birds, and the only time it sees the outside world is when it is slithering around in bird poo! The tongue-eating louse (right) is just as bad. The female louse lives in a fish's mouth, and it actually takes the place of the fish's tongue.

Animals like these are known as parasites, which means they benefit at the expense of other animals. One of the most fiendishly devious parasites is the emerald jewel wasp. It picks on the cockroach, and uses it to raise its young. The wasp's larva literally eats the roach alive and the roach can do absolutely nothing about it.

Other tiny animals are highly toxic. The Indian red scorpion is only the size of a cigarette lighter but it has enough venom to kill a human. The bullet ant has the most painful sting of any insect – it feels like being shot. Perhaps most scary of all is the giant Asian hornet. When it is not trashing honeybee hives, it's targeting humans – and killing them.

Some of these tiny terrors are devilishly cunning. The tarantula sets up trip wires with its silk to catch prey. Assassin bugs (left)and praying mantises imitate flowers and leaves before attacking their prey. And the Amazonian centipede (below) has an ingenious way of killing bats: it hangs from the ceiling of caves and catches them mid-flight.

So if you think small is beautiful, don't read any more – because we'll show you that small can be very, very dangerous.

10 THE EVIL EYE

GREEN-BANDED BROODSAC

Lenght: various)
Location: Europe and
North America

The green-banded broodsac is a flatworm, which is not the most sophisticated animal on Earth. It has no skeleton. It takes in oxygen but has no organs, such as lungs or gills, to help it breathe. It usually has an opening for taking in food, but that is exactly the same opening through which it poos!

However, in one respect, the green-banded broodsac is a smart operator.It has a very clever way of making sure it reproduces so the species survives, by spending nearly all its life inside the bodies of snails and birds.

1 The green-banded broodsac starts life as eggs in a bird. The bird poos out the eggs and, after they've landed on the ground or a tree branch, they are often consumed by nature's vacuum cleaner, the snail.

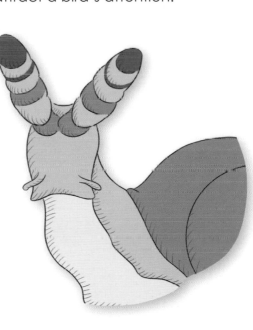

The snail can't digest the eggs. So after living in its gut for a short while, the broadsac eggs develop into miracidia (larvae) – the first stage in its development.

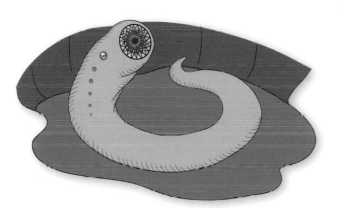

2 The miracidia wander around the snail's body and change into sporocysts. These are long tubes that can enter the snail's eyestalks. The sporocysts stretch the eyestalks and change their colour to green and yellow. For any bird that happens to be flying overhead, the snail's eyes now look like delicious morsels of caterpillar meat. The sporocysts even pulsate at a rate of 60-80 times a minute so that they attract a bird's attention.

3 Most birds would never normally go near a yucky snail, but they will gobble up the irresistible caterpillar-like eyestalks. Once swallowed by a bird, the broodsac can develop into an adult, doing little more than feeding off the food the bird eats. And, of course, it will also reproduce, sending out a stream of eggs that will be pooed out by the bird. If the poo is eaten by an unsuspecting snail, the cycle starts again!

SIZE

1

POWER

2

STRENGTH

2

AGGRESSION

2

DEADLINESS

2

TOTAL

9

9 THE CREEPY CRUSTACEAN
TONGUE-EATING LOUSE

Length: 8–29 mm (0.3–1.1 in)
Location: off the coast of Central and South America

Open wide! Now you can see the louse inside that red snapper fish. That's where it likes to live, where it's safe and can raise its young. The red snapper can't be too happy about it though. The louse has eaten its tongue and is now attached to the snapper's mouth instead.

This is the only known example of an animal replacing another animal's body part, a story that will really get tongues wagging.

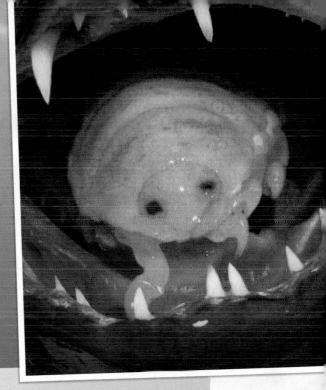

A MOTHER LOUSE IN MY MOUTH!

The tongue-eating louse is not actually a louse but a type of crustacean, just like crabs, lobsters, barnacles and shrimps. But this is a crustacean with a difference. Not only is it a blood-sucker that sets up home in a fish's mouth, it can change sex, too.

It begins life as a juvenile male trying to get into the gills of a fish. For some reason, it really likes red snappers, but it will also try this with other fish. If other lice arrive at the gills, though, the first one will become a female and crawl up through the fish's throat to the mouth. There, it attaches its seven pairs of legs to the base of the tongue, then digs its five jaws into the main part. Now it can feed off the tongue – after all, it's the tastiest part of the fish!

The next stage in the louse's life is a little mysterious. Scientists think the female mates with one of the males that were previously hanging out at the gills. The experts aren't sure exactly when the female's young are released – probably when the fish is in a school with other fish so the young lice have a good chance of finding another fish to latch on to. And if a juvenile finds a fish, the cycle can begin again. Turn to page 28 to see what happens to the adult louse and the fish.

SIZE
3
POWER
3
STRENGTH
3
AGGRESSION
5
DEADLINESS
4
TOTAL
18

DEVIL'S FLOWER PRAYING MANTIS

Length: Females – up to 13 cm (5 in);
Males – up to 10 cm (4 in)
Location: East Africa

The praying mantis gets its name from the way its forelegs are normally held: like the arms of a person praying. But the mantis is not at rest, it is ready to pounce on its prey. Should a fly, moth, butterfly or beetle stray within its view, it will swiftly seize it between the sharp spines on its forelegs. With the prey held firmly, it can bite off pieces with its jaws.

Flower mantises, such as this devil's flower mantis, are extra cunning. They disguise themselves as flowers, stalks and leaves (left), so no prey will see them before being caught.

NOT GREAT MATES

As with other species of mantis, the female devil's flower mantis will often eat the male after mating, or even during mating. She usually goes for the head first! Even if the male loses his head (literally) in the process of mating, he can still complete the act. Some male mantises try to interest the female in a courtship dance, to change her focus from feeding to mating!

STRIKING POSE

When threatened by a hungry bird or a lizard, the devil's flower mantis will try to look bigger and scarier than it really is. It raises its front legs above its head and opens them wide in what is called a deimatic display. It uses the pose to scare off predators or simply to distract them so it can make a quick getaway.

SIZE	6
POWER	3
STRENGTH	3
AGGRESSION	4
DEADLINESS	3
TOTAL	**19**

LYING IN WAIT
ASSASSIN BUGS

Length: 1–3 cm (0.4 –1.2 in)
Location: Worldwide

There are thousands of species of assassin bug, and some of them kill animals that to us are a nuisance, such as bed bugs, flies, mosquitoes and wasps as well as garden pests, such as caterpillars and beetles.

Other assassin bugs are not quite as helpful. The kissing bug comes out at night and often bites people around the mouth while they sleep. In Central and South America, it spreads the deadly Chagas disease this way!

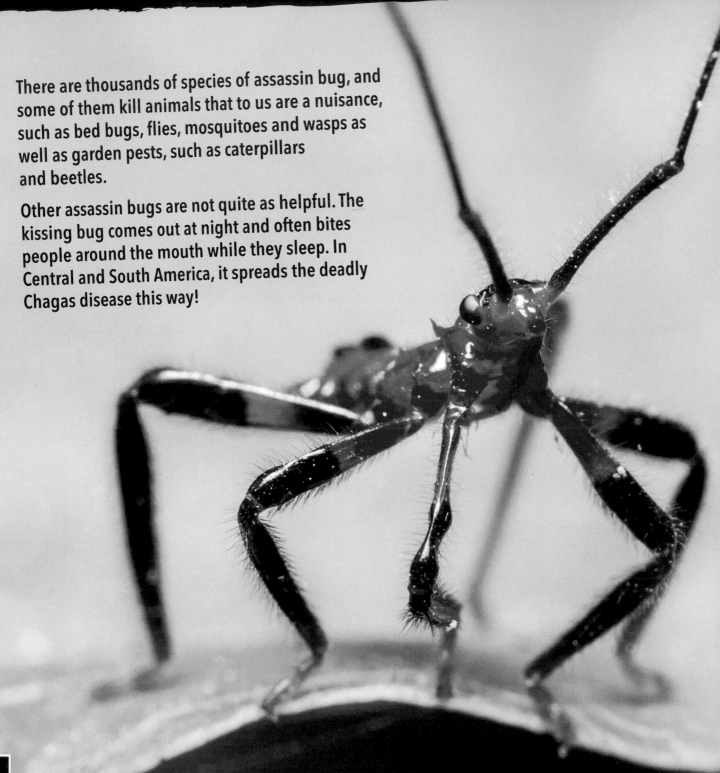

1 The milkweed assassin bug lives in North, Central and South America. It uses a 'sticky trap' strategy, hiding inside foliage with its forelegs raised in the air. They are covered with a glue-like material that traps prey.

2 Once the prey is captured, the milkweed assassin quickly punctures the body of its victim and pumps in toxic saliva. It then sucks up the insides of its prey, as if it were enjoying a drink through a straw.

3 The bug can feed on prey up to six times its own size. But the bigger the prey, the longer it takes to feed – and this means it becomes more vulnerable to other predators. So if it's too greedy, it might get eaten while it's having dinner!

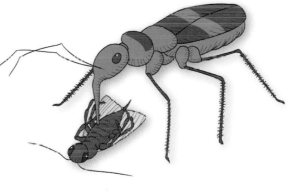

SIZE	**3**
POWER	**2**
STRENGTH	**2**
AGGRESSION	**6**
DEADLINESS	**7**
TOTAL	**20**

RED ASSASSIN BUG

The red assassin bug is common in Europe and is about 2 cm (0.8 in) long. It preys on spiders and insects, including bees and wasps. Its sting can be more painful than a bee's – so if you see one, don't touch it!

BEAUTY OR BEAST?

EMERALD JEWEL WASP

Length: up to 22 mm (0.86 in)
Location: South and Southeast Asia, Africa and the Pacific islands

Zombie cockroaches! It might sound like one of the weirdest science fiction films out there – but they really exist. The emerald jewel wasp turns cockroaches into helpless, zombified creatures to make sure its eggs turn into adults.

So if you think this wasp, with its shimmering shades of blue and green, looks stunningly beautiful, remember that for cockroaches it's a deadly enemy. Who would ever think you could feel sorry for a cockroach?

1 When the female wasp is ready to lay her eggs, she finds a cockroach – and stings it twice. The first sting temporarily paralyses the roach's front legs. The second one zombifies the cockroach – it can now feel everything, but can't defend itself or react.

2 Next the wasp grips the roach's antennae and leads it to a burrow. It is almost as if the wasp were taking a dog for a walk on a leash. The roach, in its zombified state, walks perfectly normally and fully co-operates.

3 Once inside the burrow, the wasp lays her egg on the underside of the cockroach. The wasp's work is now done and she can fly off in search of a new cockroach.

4 After a few days, the egg hatches and the larva chews its way into the roach's abdomen. It stays there for the next week, eating the roach's internal organs, on which it thrives. It changes into a pupa and, inside the roach's now dead body, it spins a cocoon and grows eyes, legs and wings. After about a month, it is ready to fly.

SIZE

3

POWER

2

STRENGTH

2

AGGRESSION

6

DEADLINESS

8

TOTAL

21

17

TOP GUN
BULLET ANT

Length: up to 25 mm (1 in)
Location: rainforests of Central and South America

What's the most painful insect sting on the planet? The common wasp or the honeybee? Not even close. The sting of the tarantula hawk wasp is a contender, but most painful of all is the bullet ant. According to victims, its sting feels like being shot, and that's how it got its name. One person described the pain even more colourfully: 'It's like fire-walking over flaming charcoal with a 3-inch rusty nail in your heel.'

NOT SO FUNNY

Australian comedian Hamish Blake tried the bullet ant gloves but could find no funny side to this story. For an hour after, he shook and sweated, stumbled and shrieked, before he called a boat to take him to the local hospital. Even after he had been given the powerful pain-killing drug morphine, he was still suffering!

RITE OF PASSAGE

In some parts of the world, it takes a lot to become a man. When boys of the Sateré-Mawé tribe in Brazil reach 13 years old, they collect bullet ants. Then a medicine man knocks out the insects with a herbal solution and weaves them inside a pair of gloves.

A boy must wear the gloves for a full 10 minutes without screaming. Remember, one ant's sting is like being shot, and there are loads of ants woven into the gloves.

SIZE

4

POWER

4

STRENGTH

3

AGGRESSION

8

DEADLINESS

7

TOTAL

26

4 BIG, HAIRY AND SCARY

TARANTULA

Length: 2.5–10 cm (1–4 in)
with leg spans of 8–30 cm (3–12 in)
Location: warm countries worldwide

Tarantulas don't use webs to capture prey like other spiders – they do it the hard way, on foot. Mind you, a web wouldn't be much use in trapping some of the animals that tarantulas like to eat, which include frogs, mice, birds and even snakes.

PARALYSING ITS PREY

A tarantula usually hunts at night, stealthily sneaking up on prey and pouncing! Its fangs are like a doctor's needle. When it bites, venom is injected through the fangs and into the victim – in this case, a tree frog. The venom paralyses the prey, and then the tarantula produces digestive juices from its mouth. These turn the frog into a soupy mess that it can easily slurp up.

SIZE

6

POWER

5

STRENGTH

5

AGGRESSION

6

DEADLINESS

5

TOTAL

27

Length: 5–9 cm (2–3.5 in)

Location: India, Pakistan, Nepal, Sri Lanka

The Indian red might not look like the scariest scorpion. It is the size of a cigarette lighter – about half as big as the world's largest scorpions. But the Indian red is a real toxic terror.

One sting can cause humans not just excruciating pain, but vomiting, breathlessness, convulsions and major heart problems. Oh, and if that isn't enough, it can also turn a victim's skin blue and make them froth at the mouth with pink slimy mucus. Without urgent treatment, it can kill.

Some scientists think that the death rate from bites of the Indian red scorpion is as high as 40%. The good news is that like other scorpions, it is actually a shy, retiring creature. However, it will attack if disturbed, and it often finds its way into houses. SInce people in Asia often wear sandals or go barefoot, the scorpion usually finds some nice exposed skin to sting.

PINCERS OR POISON

The scorpion can scuttle around quickly on its four legs, but to hunt prey it usually just lies in wait. Its large pincers are covered with tiny hairs and, as soon as an insect touches them, they come into action.

Usually, the Indian red will kill with its pincers. If this doesn't work, it has a sting in its tail – literally. The last segment, called the telson, is made up of a pair of venom glands and a barb that injects the venom. While the prey is held in the pincers, the tail curls over the body to deliver the sting.

The scorpion can only take in food in liquid form, so it cuts off a small amount of the prey with its very sharp mouth parts, known as chelicerata (chelly-sir-rata). Then it vomits digestive juices that dissolve the food. The scorpion can then suck in the liquid nourishment.

SIZE

5

POWER

5

STRENGTH

5

AGGRESSION

4

DEADLINESS

9

TOTAL

28

2 A LONG STORY

AMAZONIAN GIANT CENTIPEDE

Length: 30 cm (12 in)
Location: northern South America, Caribbean

Can you imagine this centipede creeping across the forest floor moving its legs in a wave-like rhythm in search of a tasty meal? It feeds on almost everything it can kill, including small lizards, snakes, mice and bats. The centipede is longer than an adult's forearm but some of its prey is even bigger. So what is the reason behind its hunting success? Well, it has a secret weapon: a pair of sharp claws at the front of its body. These are known as forcipules and they hold deadly venom, which leaves its prey paralysed.

DO CENTIPEDES HAVE 100 LEGS?

No. Centipedes have one pair of legs on each section of their body and they always have an odd number of sections. They might have 49 sections and 98 legs or 51 sections and 102 legs.

The Amazonian giant centipede has either 21 or 23 sections, so it has 42 or 46 legs.

SIZE

8

POWER

5

STRENGTH

6

AGGRESSION

5

DEADLINESS

7

TOTAL

31

SNAKE-EATER

Often a snake will prey on a centipede, but occasionally a centipede will manage to eat a snake. Sometimes the centipede is half the weight of the snake but if it can inject its venom near the snake's head, it will overpower it.

DEADLY WASP

ASIAN GIANT HORNET

Length: 50 mm (2 in)
Location: Eastern Asia

Who's scared of a hornet? Sure, they might give you a painful sting but they are not going to kill you, are they? Wrong. The Asian giant hornet is a real monster. It's the world's largest hornet, with a wingspan of 76 mm (3 in) – that's as wide as a baseball. And with its 6 mm (.24 in) stinger, it delivers a deadly venom that can kill a human – and it kills many every year, especially in Japan.

HAVING A BALL

Giant hornets love to attack honeybee hives and usually they create complete carnage. One hornet can tear apart up to 40 honeybees every minute, leaving a pile of severed heads and wings in its wake. However, Japanese honeybees have an amazing defensive strategy. Hundreds of them will swarm over the hornet intruder and hold it in a tight ball. When the temperature rises to 47°C (117°F), the hornet gets roasted to death.

SIZE	4
POWER	7
STRENGTH	6
AGGRESSION	9
DEADLINESS	8
TOTAL	34

GREEN-BANDED BROODSAC

Snails infected with the green-banded broodsac tend to come out in the open. Scientists believe the broodsac takes control of the snail's brain and forces it into the open. Why? It is easier for birds to see them and eat them!

TONGUE-EATING LOUSE

Once the female louse has released her young from inside the fish's mouth, her job is done. She either floats away or gets swallowed by the fish. Unfortunately, the fish's fate is sealed, as it cannot survive without a tongue!

EMERALD JEWEL WASP

The emerald jewel wasp is solitary and, like all other adult wasps, it is unable to eat solid food. It relies on sucking or drinking the hemolymph (blood) of cockroaches and other insects. The female wasps lay dozens of eggs in different coachroaches.

BULLET ANT

Bullet ants live in large colonies containing up to several hundred individuals. They usually build nests at the bottom of tall trees, and include chambers with domed ceilings. Often the chamber walls will be lined with plant matter that the worker ants have foraged.

AMAZONIAN GIANT CENTIPEDE

The Amazonian centipede is the longest centipede on Earth but it's nowhere near the leggiest. The *Gonibregmatus plurimipes* from Fiji in the Pacific Ocean has 382 legs! The leggiest creature of all is a millipede. The *Illacme plenipes* lives in California and, at 3cm (1.2 in), is much smaller than your little finger. But the females still manage to have up to 750 legs.

DEVIL'S FLOWER PRAYING MANTIS

The praying mantis is the only invertebrate (animal without a backbone) to be able to see in 3D. It has five eyes – two large ones and three smaller ones in between.

ASSASSIN BUG

A West African assassin bug carries the remains of the ants, termites and flies it has eaten on its back – a 'backpack' of carcasses. If a predator tries its luck, it is likely to end up with a mouthful of dead insects, instead of the assassin bug.

TARANTULA

After mating, female tarantulas lay hundreds of eggs and encase them in a silken sac that they spin. They guard the eggs aggressively and occasionally turn them over with their jaws to help brood them. If distressed, however, they sometimes eat the eggs.

INDIAN RED SCORPION

Scorpions are among the oldest land animals, dating back about 400 million years. The first scorpions, however, were sea scorpions. Closely related to the land variety, they could grow to an amazing 2.5 m (8 ft) long and had vicious claws the size of tennis rackets.

ASIAN GIANT HORNET

Giant hornets tend to attack honeybee nests in autumn when they are rearing queens and males in their nests. After a successful attack, the hornets will chew up the bodies of the honeybee larvae and pupae, and take them back to their hive to feed their own larvae. Hornet workers will retrieve food from the honeybee hive for up to two weeks.

ALL IN A DAY'S WORK

In bullet ant society, smaller workers stay inside the nest and tend the queen and her eggs, while larger ones forage and defend the nest. The foragers often venture as far as the canopy – 40 metres (130 ft) above ground. They collect nectar, the sugar-rich liquid produced by plants, as well as small insects, such as termites, other smaller ants and even wasps.

These ants take the food back to the nest in their mandibles, a pair of claw-like limbs near their mouth. They can even carry liquid droplets without bursting them. Everything is shared with the other ants and larvae inside the nest.

WILY WAYS

Assassin bugs use some very crafty hunting strategies. An Australian bug will hang out in a spider's web, plucking the strands. When the spider comes to see if it's caught some prey, it becomes the prey for the bug.

A Costa Rican bug hunts termites. It knows that they will remove dead termites from their nest to keep it disease-free. So once the assassin bug has caught one termite and sucked it dry, it dangles the remains into the termite nest. When another termite comes to clear up the dead body, the assassin bug captures this new victim. One assassin bug was seen using this trick to capture 48 termites in a single sitting!

CENTIPEDES OR MILLIPEDES?

Centipedes and millipedes are both myriapods. So what's the difference between them? The main one is that millipedes have two pairs of legs on each section of their body, while centipedes have just one pair on each section. Millipedes also tend to feed off decaying plant matter, whereas nearly all centipedes – like the Amazonian giant – are predators. As a result, centipedes generally move more quickly because they have to chase prey.

The oldest known land animal, *Pneumodesmus newmani*, was a myriapod that existed 428 million years ago. And if you think the Amazonian giant centipede is a good size at 30 cm (12 in), that's nothing compared to the arthropleura millipede. It lived around 320 million years ago and measured 2.6 metres (8.5 ft): as long as two full-size bicycles!

THE HUMAN KILLER

The giant hornet is certainly not afraid of humans. Each year in Japan it kills around 30 to 40 people. In 2013 in Shaanxi province, China, it killed at least 42 people and injured more than 1,600 others. One victim told the local media: 'The more you run, the more they want to chase you.' And some victims described being chased for about 200 metres (656 ft). The giant hornet is no slouch; it can fly up to 40 km/h (25 mph).

However, humans do get their own back. The hornet is a delicacy in mountain villages in Japan, eaten either raw (hornet sashimi) or deep-fried. Bon appetit!

INDEX

THE AUTHOR
Matthew Rake lives in London and has worked in publishing for more than twenty years. He has written on a wide variety of topics including science, sports, and the arts.

THE ARTIST
Award-winning illustrator Simon Mendez combines his love of nature and drawing by working as an illustrator with a focus on scientific and natural subjects. He paints on a wide variety of themes but mainly concentrates on portraits and animal subjects. He lives in the United Kingdom.

Picture Credits (abbreviations: t = top; b = bottom; c = centre; l = left; r = right)

© www.shutterstock.com: 1c, 3c, 5b, 6l, 8, 12l, 14, 15br, 16, 18bl, 20, 21tr, 22, 25tr, 28tl, 28cl, 28cr, 28b, 29tl, 29tr, 29cl, 29cr, 29b, 30tr, 30bl, 32r.